Creating Colour

with

Airbrush paints

by

Dawn Butler

Creating Colour with Airbrush paints
By Dawn Butler

Design © 131 Design Ltd

Text & images © Dawn Butler

ISBN 978-1-909660-19-9
A CIP catalogue record for
this book is available from
the British Library.

Published 2013 by Tricorn Books,
a trading name of 131 Design Ltd.
131 High Street, Old Portsmouth,
PO1 2HW
www.tricornbooks.co.uk
Printed & bound in UK by W&G Baird

Splats are to be used as a guide only. They are a visual representation of the colour that can be achieved. To seek an accurate colour match please refer to the Pantone® code on the right hand column. All Pantone® codes in this book refer to Pantone® solid coated colours. Pantone® is the universal colour reference chart that is used to catalogue and match colour

Meet Dawn Butler, founder of Dinkydoodle Designs. When she isn't busy being a wife, and mother to her young family, she spends her days designing and creating cakes, developing exciting new and innovative cake craft products, and teaching her novelty cake and airbrushing skills around the globe! In just three years, Dawn has gained the recognition of being one of the world's leading cake specialists and has a growing number of followers – all wondering what on earth she will come up with next! But how did it all begin?

Dawn found her passion for cake decorating almost 20 years ago when she took a job in a local bakery. It was a short 6-week summer holiday job, but it sparked something inside that would burn for many years to come. After finishing university Dawn joined the police force and enjoyed a successful career. It wasn't until 10 years later that she returned to cake decorating, when she began to create cakes for her own children. In 2010 she was persuaded to turn her love of cakes into a business, and using the pet name her Mum and Dad gave her, "Dinkydoodle" Designs was born!

You can look at her creations, get in touch or follow her progress on either Facebook or Twitter.

You can also read her blogs at www.dinkydoodle.co.uk

There is always something going on, so what are you waiting for? Stop by and say hello!

To buy a Dinkydoodle product visit:
www.dinkydoodledesigns.co.uk or keep up to date at:

 Twitter: @dinkydoodlecake

 Facebook: Dinkydoodle Designs by Dawn Butler

Contents

Introduction

When producing a cake, whether for a customer, competition or showpiece, there is always a lot of thought that goes into the colour of it. I *LOVE* colour, but what I love even more, is the possibility of making cakes that look like something else! Whether that is a cooked breakfast, naughty puppy, allotment vegetables, or a life size boy - I never tire of hearing people ask . .   . "Is that cake?"

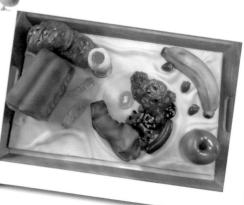

Ok, so I know a little bit about cake and can carve and cover a cake nicely, but what brings them to life is the finish, and for me, this is almost always achieved through airbrushing.

I am always challenging myself to see what I can achieve in cake. Since having my own range of airbrush paints, I have found that even more is possible when I let loose and experiment. Indeed some of my most successful discoveries have come from happy accidents!

I have lost count of the times that someone has asked me, "How did you achieve that colour?" or "What colours have you used there?" My colours are so different to anything else on the market, it allows me to achieve such a wide range of colours and effects that I often have people wondering just how I've done it.

Now don't get me wrong, I love sharing my information, but when I tell people how to mix them to achieve a specific result, a daunted look appears on their face as they don't feel confident in remembering the colour sequence, or are afraid of trying at home.

So after many months of mixing, spraying, testing and cataloguing I have produced this unique guide to mixing the Dinkydoodle Paints. It has been designed as a notebook, a user-friendly workbook to  have along side you as you experiment and create.

You may use it just as you like, but there are a few things about it which are certain. It is NOT precious. It will NOT look pretty on your shelf and it serves NO purpose in your cupboard. It is equally by no means a definitive guide - I think I could have mixed colours everyday for a decade and still come up with something new!

Firstly, please USE it, have FUN with it, let it help and inspire you but most of all, let it give you confidence to take things further, mixing your own colours to create amazing cakes.

When I'm working I am often surrounded by colour swatches, mood scenes or photographs to help inspire me and I have therefore left some space in this book for you to make your own notes on the colours you discover, allowing you to record their recipe and replicate them easily time after time.

Lastly, ENJOY it. I am immensely proud of my first book. It was a pleasure to share my passion with you. It has taken me on a journey, where I have learned so much about colour, how to mix it, use it and choose others that compliment it. I hope that you get as much enjoyment out of using it as I did from writing it.

Yours

Dawn Butler
Dinkydoodle Designs

The Theory of Colour

If we take ourselves back to our school days most of us can remember what the primary colours are, but after that everything gets a little fuzzy.

Whilst I don't want to labour the many elements of colour theory, as I am certainly not a scholar on the subject, it is important that we appreciate the principles of it, in order that we understand not only how to mix colours, but also how to choose complimentary colours when selecting a colour scheme. To do this I will refer to the artists' colour wheel. There are several types of colour wheel - some having different sets of colour - but the artists' colour wheel is the most relevant for our needs.

The Colour Wheel

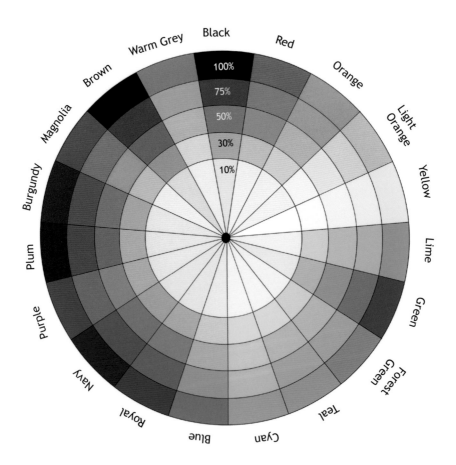

A comprehensive colour wheel containing primary, secondary and tertiary colours, along with blacks and greys and the varying tones in each colour hue.

The Beginning –
The Primary Colours

In the first instance there are three primary colours. These three colours cannot be made from any other colours. Instead they are a source of all other colours.

Secondary Colours

There are also 3 secondary colours. These are made when 2 primary colours are mixed together. For example, red and yellow make orange, yellow and blue make green and so on.

Tertiary Colours

Finally, for now at least, come tertiary colours. These are colours that come from mixing a primary and secondary colour together, or by mixing two secondary colours together.

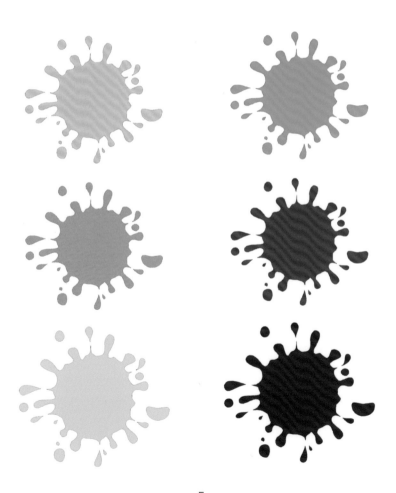

I could go on for hours with all sorts of colour information on shades, tints, tones and hues, as this is just the tip of the iceberg, but I will be covering more on the subject later. So for now, we should have at least created a very basic colour wheel and it should look something like this.

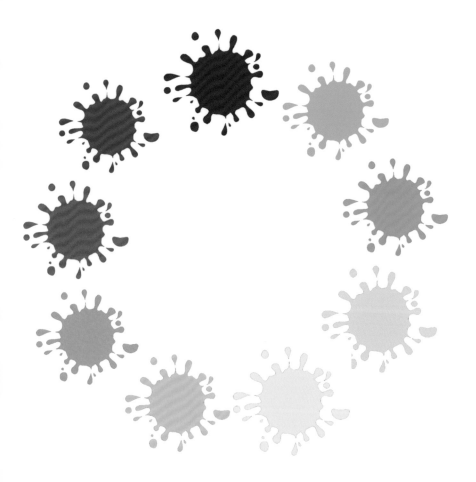

Dinkydoodle Paints

So what makes my colours different from all the others on the market? Some of you may have already noticed but most other airbrush colours you can buy are water based. When you look at them they are translucent; they have the appearance of coloured water.

Dinkydoodle Paints on the other hand are opaque in appearance and rather than being water based, are made with an ethanol and powder mixture, which behaves entirely differently when used in an airbrush.

For those seasoned cake decorators amongst us, you will know that water is not a preferred medium to be used on a cake, as it can cause pitting (if splattered for instance) and staining of the sugar paste. Many cake decorators therefore use a clear alcohol on cakes (as an adhesive etc), as when it dries it leaves no marks behind, as the alcohol evaporates in the air.

My colours work on the same principle. Ethanol, which is a food safe, factory produced ingredient (with the same properties as alcohol) is used as the propellant for the colour and when it leaves the airbrush in a fine mist of spray it starts to evaporate in the air, even before hitting the cake.

This leaves the powder particles of colour behind, giving a powder coat finish to the cake, which is almost dry to the touch immediately after spraying.

As a pleasant surprise when first using these products, I discovered the colours would layer on top of each other without having any colour changing effect; much like you would expect with oil or acrylic paints when one colour is painted over another after the first one is dry. This is the result of the evaporation and powder coat finish.

But why is that significant?

Well, if you remember our colour wheel, you will remember that when we mix two primary colours, another colour is created, and with water based airbrush colours this is done by either mixing the two colours together before spraying or afterwards when spraying one on top of the other.

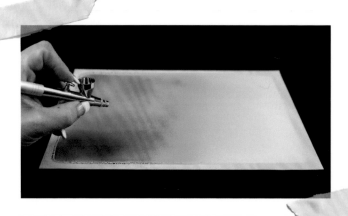

This is not necessarily a problem, although it does place huge restrictions on what you can achieve when airbrushing on cakes as you have to plan out, not only every colour to be used, but also the order you want to use them in, and mask your work off accordingly if you do not want any over-spray to effect the finished result. For instance, how many of us have ever airbrushed a blue sky on a cake, then decided it needed a yellow sun, only to find the sun turns green?

So wouldn't it be nice to use colour like an artist, and not be restricted to selecting only one or two colours for a cake for fear of making a mess of the whole thing through over-spray? Or, you have had to design your cake so that each element is sprayed separately, to avoid all the colours merging into one? Well that is precisely what you can do with Dinkydoodle Paints! If you spray blue on top of yellow, you get blue and yellow, you can even spray light onto dark. In fact any colour combination you choose for a cake is now possible with Dinkydoodle Paints. The only limit to your creation will be your imagination!

Whilst this book is all about colour, it is also worth mentioning that another great benefit of the colours' ability to layer is that it will sit on just about any surface (I haven't found one yet that I cant airbrush!), and by that I mean my paints will spray, not only onto sugar paste, but also marzipan, butter cream, biscuits, chocolate, ice cream, jelly, jams and preserves, and also real fruit such as apples and strawberries! You can have great fun airbrushing all sorts of things, and no longer need to limit yourself to cake as your creative medium. I feel a whole other book coming on, for that topic!

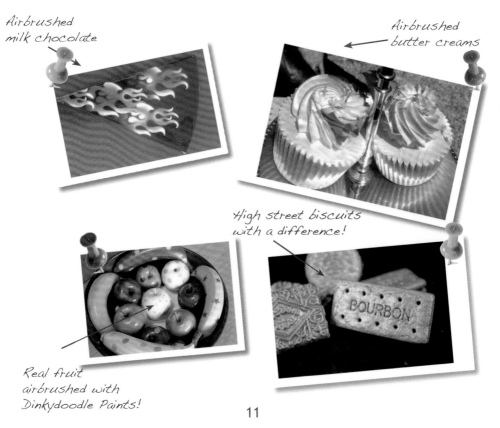

Airbrushed milk chocolate

Airbrushed butter creams

High street biscuits with a difference!

Real fruit airbrushed with Dinkydoodle Paints!

Different Paint Finishes

The three main finishes are Matt, Pearl and Iridescent. The picture below shows three roses, each of which have been sprayed in the three different finishes of the same colour. You can immediately see the difference. The matt blue on the left, is as you expect it to be, a full, base colour with an egg shell finish. The middle rose is sprayed with my blue pearl colour - you can see how this one catches the light and has a lustre finish that you would expect from a pearlised colour. Finally on the right is iridescent blue.

The edges of this rose have been gently sprayed with black first so that you can clearly see the iridescent effect.

These selections of colours are truly amazing and have to be seen if they're to be really appreciated. I will cover them in more detail later but in brief, they are a true metallic colour, in that they are an iridescent overlay - an interference colour. This means that they will reflect the light (appearing to change the colour dependent on the angle it is viewed at) but will not cover or mask the base colour that they are sprayed on to.

But if all my colours stay true when you overlay them (i.e. blue and yellow won't turn green), what happens when you want them to mix? For this there is a simple solution. You simply mix them together in a bottle prior to spraying . . . and that's what's this book is all about!

Shall we get started?

Basic Mixing - *tools and rules*

I say rules, but they're more guidelines really. They are little tips that will make colour mixing easier for you. The most important of them being:

Measure what you want to mix!

If you are to have any hope of replicating the colours you make, you need to know how you did it. If you haven't measured it - just adopted the splash of this, dash of that formula - you my end up wasting a lot of colour in the future when you come to try and make it again. (Or end up with an excess of varying shades of brown, as over mixing invariably seems to end up this colour!)

Record what you have mixed!

Just as important as the first tip: if you don't record what you have measured, how are you going to remember it? (I struggle remembering what I had for breakfast, let alone the colour recipe of each shade of colour I create.) I have given you space in the back of this book to record your own creations, but when you are recording it's important to always use the same formula.

Tools for the job

When deciding on what are the best tools to measure out colour, I thought of several ways to do this, from nifty gizmos and gadgets to special bottles with lines and markings. In the end I opted for an explanation on how I measure them, using the very thing that comes with the colour - the lid of the bottle itself. (Referred to as the cap for measuring purposes in this book.)

It doesn't actually matter which cap you use either. For instance you may decant your colours into your own favourite style bottles that you have saved and stored from another purpose, as long as you always use the same sized cap for all your measurements (when a cap measurement is required).

The only other measuring tool I use is a pipette (or dropper), which I use when I only need a tiny amount of colour (usually when adding black) to a recipe. If you have a Dinkydoodle Airbrush you will have received one in the box but they are also available to buy through my website or other stockist of Dinkydoodle products. (See the stockist list at the rear of this book.)

Colour mixing conversion chart

Measuring tool used in this book	Is also equal to:
Cap from a Dinkydoodle colour bottle	5ml of fluid
Pipette dropper	100 drops equals 1 cap

Dinkydoodle paints

Stickers to label your bottled creations

Caps to bottles used in measurements

Pippette for smaller measurements

Old paintbrushes or sticks for mixing

You can use the cap of any bottle, but for each recipe use the same cap

16

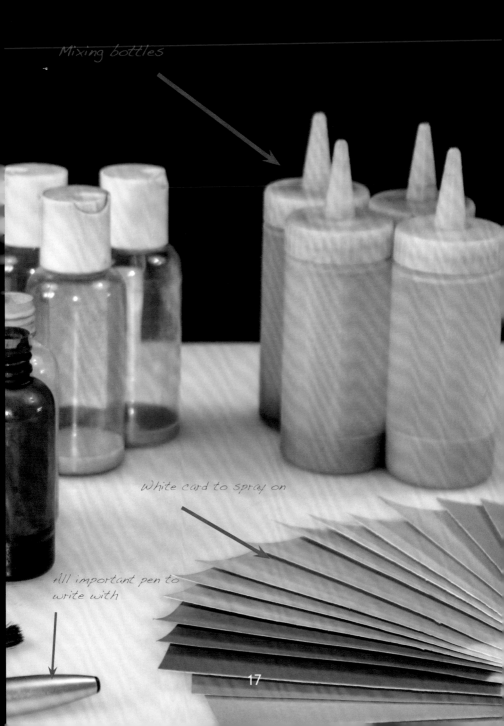

Mixing bottles

White card to spray on

All important pen to
write with

17

How to mix and record your colours using ratios

There is an easy way to record your recipes that will allow you to scale the quantity of colour mixed up or down depending on the volume of colour you wish to mix. (2 caps full of colour may not be enough for your project.) Whilst you may physically work in caps full of colour (certainly the first time you mix it and whilst you're experimenting, so as not to waste too much colour when things don't turn out as planned). If you think of each cap as a portion of colour it will allow you to mix it in larger quantities once you are satisfied with your creation. These portions are known as a *Ratio* - a particular measurement of colour used in your recipe. Ratio doesn't refer to the size of it, but explains how many portions are required of that particular colour. It can easily be explained in the pie chart on the next page.

As you can see from the charts, the recipe to make the colours is simple whether it be of equal parts (1:1), a 2:1 ratio or in multi-colour mixing where the ratio of several colours is involved (2:1:1).

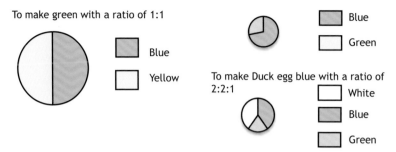

To make green with a ratio of 1:1

Blue

Yellow

Blue

Green

To make Duck egg blue with a ratio of 2:2:1

White

Blue

Green

Once you have actually made your desired colour and recorded it, you may want to store it for future use, particularly if you haven't used it all on your project. I have a range of plastic bottles for this purpose which are easy to pour from and also allow me to see what colour is inside. I also label mine with address labels, containing colour ratios and the name I have given it for easy reference.

So for the purposes of this book, all the recipes for the colours will be measured in either caps: a full cap of colour filled to the brim or drops: a pipette full of colour. I find it easiest to pour colour into the cap first and then squeeze the pipette gently to release one drop of colour at a time. There is a useful conversion chart at the rear of this book that converts caps and drops into other recognised measurements.

Note: this then needs adding to the rear of the book and also to the contents page, with relevant page number.

The final tip on mixing is . . .

Start with the lightest colour first!

When mixing colours you must always remember that the colour you start with, will affect the colour at the end, for instance it is far easier to darken or change the shade of a light colour, than it is to lighten a dark one.

A perfect example of this is grey

To achieve an effective grey, most people think that you start with black (particularly if you are making a dark grey). In reality black is such a dark base that when you add the amount of white you think would be right for the colour, it doesn't actually make grey at all, but instead a random shade of blue.

However, if you're to start with white and add only drops of black (because it is such a strong colour), you will be able to control the change in colour until the desired grey is achieved. There is a whole section later on how to mix different tones of grey.

10%   100% Black

Two colour mixing

Going back to our colour wheel again, two-colour mixing is where it all begins - mixing 2 of the primary colours together to create another colour. And bearing our rule in mind about starting with the lightest colour, it would be wise to start with yellow and add a small amount of red hoping to get a deep orange.

Let's have a look at how the basic secondary colours are achieved.

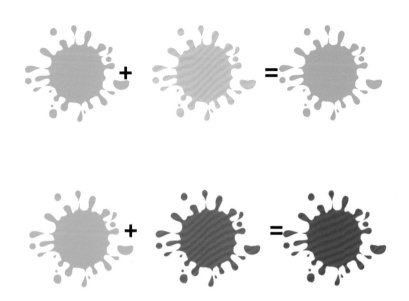

Of course these have been made using equal quantities of each (1:1) but you don't have to stick with this, you may want to adjust your ratios accordingly for the particular colour that you require. For instance, here are the same mix of colours but this time the ratios have been changed.

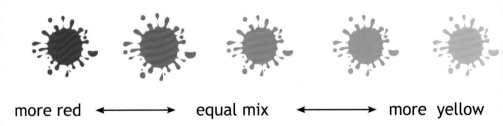

more red ←——→ equal mix ←——→ more yellow

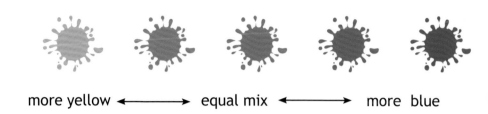

more yellow ←——→ equal mix ←——→ more blue

more red ←——→ equal mix ←——→ more blue

And remember, two-colour mixing doesn't have to be just between 2 primary colours, a combination of primary, secondary or tertiary colours can also be used.

Multi-colour mixing

As the name suggest, this is where more than 2 colours are used in combination to create your desired colour. The ratio element is still relevant, in fact even more so. It is critical that you record the amounts for each colour you add as any alteration in this area will affect the overall outcome. It is also worth noting that the order you add them to the mix may alter the outcome too. (See mixing rules and tools for more details.)

Tones, Tints, Shades and Hues

These words are often used in sentences to describe colours but how many of us I wonder actually know what they mean? (I know that I didn't truly understand until recently!)

So what do they mean? And what is the difference between them?

A Hue

This is the term used for a full colour, the basic colours on the colour wheel. The three primary colours are perfect examples of this.

A Tint

This is the result of any colour, (whether mixed or primary) that has been made lighter by adding white.

A Shade

Is the opposite of a tint, whereby the colour has been made darker by adding black to it.

A Tone

A particular colour can be made a different "tone" of colour by adding grey to it.

The Colour Charts

Number	Ratio colour mix	Pantone code
1	yellow 1 white 1	135 C
2	yellow 1 white 1 orange 1	150C
3	yellow 1 white 1 orange 1 red 1	7580 C
4	yellow 1 white 1 orange 1 red 1 purple 1	4985 C

Number	Ratio colour mix	Pantone code	
1	yellow 1 green 1	618 C	
2	yellow 1 green 1 white 1	7508 C	
3	yellow 1 green 1 white 1 blue 1	625 C	
4	yellow 1 green 1 white 1 blue 1 purple 1	5483 C	

Number	Ratio colour mix	Pantone code
1	yellow 1 orange 1	715 C
2	yellow 1 orange 1 red 1	7619C
3	yellow 1 orange 1 red 1 pink 1	7418 C
4	yellow 1 orange 1 red 1 pink 1 white 1	7416C
5	yellow 1 orange 2 red 1 pink 1 white 2	162C

Number	Ratio colour mix	Pantone code
1	orange 3 red 1	7417C
2	orange 3 red 1 brown 1	492C
3	orange 3 red 1 brown 1 yellow 1	7592C
4	orange 3 red 1 brown 2 yellow 1	7581C
5	orange 3 red 1 brown 2 yellow 1 purple 1	4705C

Number	Ratio colour mix	Pantone code
1	red 2 blue 1	5395C
2	red 2 blue 1 pink 1	5265C
3	red 2 blue 1 pink 1 purple 1	5275C
4	red 2 blue 1 pink 1 purple 1 white 1	7667C
5	red 3 blue 1 pink 1 purple 1 white 1	5195 C

Number	Ratio colour mix	Pantone code
1	pink 1 white 1	7612C
2	pink 1 red 1	702C
3	pink 1 red 2	7419C
4	pink 1 red 1 purple 1	5195C
5	pink 1 red 1 purple 1 white 1	5205C

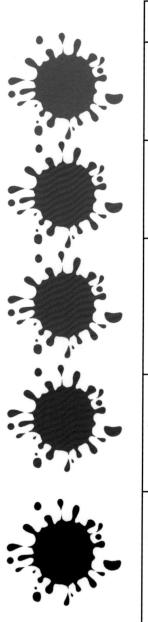

Number	Ratio colour mix	Pantone code
1	pink 1 red 1 black 1	437C
2	pink 1 purple 1	7665C
3	pink 1 purple 1 red 1	4985C
4	pink 2 purple 2 red 2 black 1	5195C
5	pink 2 purple 2 red 2 black 2	5185C

Number	Ratio colour mix	Pantone code
1	blue 1 green 1	7716C
2	blue 1 green 2	569C
3	blue 1 green 2 white 1	2243C
4	blue 1 green 2 white 2	3265C
5	blue 1 green 2 white 3 yellow 1	367C

Number	Ratio colour mix	Pantone code
1	blue 2 green 1	3288c
2	blue 2 green 3	7716C
3	blue 2 green 3 white 1	7472C
4	blue 2 green 3 white 3	325 C
5	blue 2 green 3 white 5	3242C

Number	Ratio colour mix	Pantone code
1	green 2 blue 3 black 1	7475C
2	green 2 blue 3 black 1 white 1	7696C
3	green 2 blue 3 white 2 black 1	7459C
4	blue 3 green 2 black 1 white 1 purple 1	7706C
5	blue 3 green 2 black 1 purple 1 white 2	7681C

Number	Ratio colour mix	Pantone code
1	yellow 1 brown 1	7519C
2	yellow 2 brown 1	876C
3	yellow 2 brown 1 white 1	479C
4	yellow 2 brown 1 white 1 orange 1	1605C
5	yellow 2 brown 1 white 2 orange 1 pink 1	7591C

Number	Ratio colour mix	Pantone code
1	brown 1 white 2	7615 C
2	yellow 2 brown 1 white 3 orange 1 pink 3	473C
3	yellow 2 brown 1 white 3 orange 1 pink 2	721C
4	yellow 3 brown 1 white 3 orange 1 pink 1	719C
5	yellow 3 brown 1 white 5 orange 1 pink 1	482C

Number	Ratio colour mix	Pantone code
1	green 2 purple 1	5477C
2	green 2 purple 1 black 1	5473C
3	green 2 purple 1 red 1	5545C
4	green 3 black 1	7736C
5	green 3 navy blue 1	3302C

Number	Ratio colour mix	Pantone code
1	white 5 caps: black 15 drops	420 C
2	white 5 caps: black 45 drops	423C
3	white 5 caps: black 200 drops	cool grey 11 C
4	white 5 caps: black 100 drops	445
5	white 5 caps: black 300 drops	7450 C

Special Finishes

All of the colours mixed so far have been done using the Matt Dinkydoodle range but there are so many other colours and effects that can be created by using the colours from my Pearl and Iridescent colour range.

The principles are the same although the base colours for the pearl range are different, so when you mix the pearl colours do not expect the same results as the Matt.

For an example of this let's look at the basic difference between Pearl pink and Matt pink.

If we were trying to mix a colour that required matt pink (for example), but we did it with pearl pink instead, we couldn't expect the same outcome because the base is different.

With that in mind, if you are using pearl colours as your base for mixing be aware that your ratios may need to be altered accordingly - you may even need to add white to lighten them and more experimenting may be required.

You of course don't have to start with 2 pearl colours, you can mix any combination of finishes to get your desired colour, and mixing pearl and a matt may be preferable to you due to the tint or shade of the base colour. Don't forget though that if only one pearl colour is used in the mix, it will lessen the overall effectiveness of the pearl finish and the ratio of pearl used will highlight this fact even more. For example if a colour contains a ratio of 1:3, 1 part pearl yellow to 3 parts matt blue, the colour you achieve will be a shade of green, but don't expect it to have a pearlised finish

So how can I make any colour I mix, a pearlised colour?

This can be done in 2 ways and by experimenting for yourself, it will allow you to decide which method is best for you.

The first is by simply spraying your project in one colour and then over spraying it with pearl.

If you try this method you will notice that because the colours will over spray each other without mixing, it does affect the colour, especially the more coats of pearl you spray on top.

The second is by mixing pearl in with the colour when you make it. But don't forget - pearl has a white base to it and will lighten any colour you mix.

If you remember back to the section about tints, shades and tones, a colour that has been made lighter with white is a now a tint of that particular colour.

After you've added pearl to your mix, you may find it is now too light for your purpose so you may need to combat that by adding a small amount of grey or black to darken it again. Like I said, you may need to experiment for yourself to ensure it suits your specific needs but the above points are worth bearing in mind, particularly if you're trying to match a specific colour and you're wondering why it is lighter than expected.

Iridescent Colours

As I mentioned before, these are something very special. A unique range of colours that will allow you to access a whole colour spectrum that was impossible before.

My Iridescent range is simply a lustre with an ethanol propellant. There is no pigment base to them and therefore they behave in a very different way.

I used to label this range as metallic to suggest how it should be used. One definition of a metallic colour is that they are interference colours, an iridescent overlay, which change the appearance of the base colour dependent on how the light reflects upon it.

If you have experienced the colours in this range before you will understand how well this definition fits. However, how many of us really study the information on the label for the products we buy?

For some, the title "metallic" puts a picture in their mind of a shiny red sports car - and they wouldn't be wrong. But in respect of the Dinkydoodle Paint range, there is a little more to it than that.

This cake has actually been done with my red matt paint and finished with several coats of

my shell and shine spray, (my own brand of edible varnish.)

I think you'll agree the colour looks great, and it may look like what you perceive to be a metallic colour (because it's on a car cake) but in reality, achieving this particular result had nothing to do with metallic colours at all.

In their basic form, when sprayed on white sugar paste (or anything else white), they will create a delicate lustre of whatever shade you have chosen. Such as gold, blue, green and rose (used to be called red) they are perfect for wedding cakes, fairy wings and fantasy flowers, and always remind me of mother of pearl.

Photo above taken by Clark Stanley-Smith for Cake Craft and Decoration Monthly Magazine and is published in this book with their kind permission. The carved car cake can be seen in full step-by-step detail in their June 2013 edition.

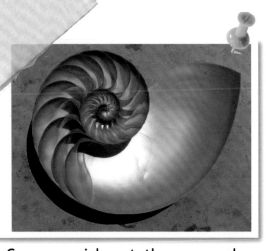

To show you how they would look if sprayed on top of each other on a white background, have a look at this shell. Can you pick out the rose colour, blue, green and gold? This is how they look when used on white, a very delicate colour that really stands out when it catches the light. How many of you, have tried to add lustre dust to a cake to give it a gold shimmer, not wanting to change the base colour of the cake, but struggled to get the lustre powder evenly spread? If you're anything like me, you may have ended up with a large clump where you have tried to brush it around the cake.

Well, with the iridescent paints you can achieve this look in seconds and because you are airbrushing it on, you get an even more subtle coat of lustre without all of the bother and mess. But that is only the beginning. . . . My iridescent paints do not mask the base colour you have used. Instead, they enhance it. Your colour combinations of iridescent over other colours will evolve your colours into something truly spectacular.

When I use the iridescent colours I tend not to use the same colour iridescent over the same base colour. For instance, if I spray blue iridescent over blue matt you will not see any real difference,(you would be as well to use blue pearl). But when you start to combine the colours and for instance, spray blue iridescent over red matt you will actually create a colour that looks like ultra violet purple.

And what happens when you spray them onto a black surface? It's these results that still amaze me even now.

When I'm teaching I demonstrate with my colours to explain how they work and how people can get the most of out them. Students are pleased when I pass round an example of the iridescent sprayed onto white, and I can see the cogs turning as to how each of them may use them. I then get out something covered in black sugar paste and

spray it over with an iridescent colour and the room is a gasp with the result. It's something I never tire from.

The first thing that springs to my mind when I see the blue and the green (and even the gold for that matter), is how, blended together you could create the most life like and stunning peacock colour or perhaps a scarab beetle.

And I have yet to find a customer that needs a cake made to look like Paua shell - but I can assure you, when they do I'm ready, armed with my iridescent range.

I am yet to exhaust the colour combinations with the iridescent range. Why don't you have some fun with them and see what you get up to?

Colours of Metal

Everyone in the cake world is always after easy and effective ways to create gold, silver, copper and bronze. Well, look no further than this section because with Dinkydoodle Paints it couldn't be any easier! Whilst I sell a gold pearl already (so no need to make one), it is still worthy of mention here as to how it can be used to great effect when mixing.

Already there are 2 shades of gold available to you: one is the gold pearl straight from the bottle and the second is gold iridescent when sprayed over black. (See the section in iridescent colours.)

Gold iridescent sprayed on to a black surface.

Gold pearl sprayed on to a white surface.

In actual fact, there is also a third. My Dinkydoodle Yellow pearl is a very rich yellow, and because it is a pearlised colour it can give the impression of being gold, (particularly if sprayed onto a darker background).

48

Yellow pearl sprayed on to a white surface

Yellow pearl sprayed on to a black surface.

And last, but by no means least, silver. I can't tell you how many times I have been asked what colours to use to make true silver. So many that I have now given my recipe to the factory for them to bottle as ready-made. But this book is about how to mix colours (from the smaller range you may already have) so it is certainly useful to show you how to make it for yourself. (Also how to change the shade etc.)

Like the iridescent colours, my pearl colour can appear very different when sprayed onto a white background or when sprayed onto a darker background.

The rose below is my pearl colour when sprayed onto white sugar paste. You can see instantly that there is a lot of lustre to it (to give the pearlised finish) but the colour remains white.

Just look at what happens when you spray the same pearl colour onto a black surface. This was done with just one coat of pearl on top of an airbrushed black surface. You can of course change the tone of silver by either adding more coats of

pearl, starting with a shade of grey or choosing to mix your colours together before spraying.

Verdigris

I love verdigris. It's such an unusual finish. The colours are a perfect compliment to each other; I love the way that one peeps out from behind the other.

In real life of course, the effect has been created by an item that is made of copper (usually a  statue) being weathered and affected by the elements. When this happen the copper turns green and you are left with 2 beautiful colours - the beautiful base copper and the stunning light blue/green on the surface.

I have always fancied re-creating this effect but until now it was not possible for me to do . . . until the Dinkydoodle paints that is!

It is so simple. First use my Dinkydoodle copper to cover your whole project. Secondly, spray the covered project with a light coat of my shell and shine spray (edible varnish). For this project it works as a sealant and allows you to create the overall effect. Now spray your project all over with your chosen shade of blue/green. (I used my duck egg blue on page 34 row 5). Because you have protected the base layer with a coat of varnish you will now be able to rub off parts of the new top coat of colour. If you hadn't, you run the risk of wiping both sets of colours off and returning your project back to white.

A moulded item or something with texture, is perfect for this effect, as you can rub gently with kitchen towel (or a dry sponge), to take off small areas of the top coat and expose the copper underneath. Simple! Why not give it a go and see what you can create!

This is my bronze colour on a white surface. And for the right hand rose, this is my Copper colour on a white surface.

Choosing and Creating a Colour scheme

Part of what makes a stunning cake is the colours that have been used as part of it. There is something about a good colour scheme that connects with the brain to make it pleasing to the eye.

For those skilled in colour theory, colours are not selected by accident and it is often something as simple as well used colour that makes their cakes stand out from others.

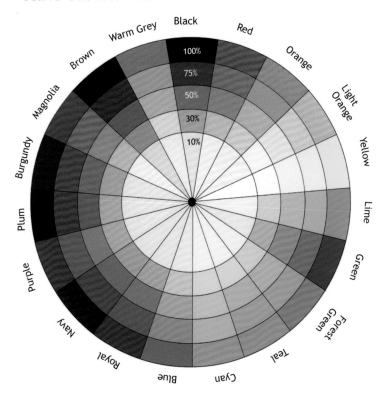

Analogous colour schemes

For a colour scheme that contains minimal colour contrast, you would simply choose three adjacent colours in the colour wheel. The only rule here is that they must be of the same saturation (or hue). It wouldn't look right to use a hue of one colour, a tint of a second colour and a tone of a third – (see this section for more details). This colour combination is called an analogous colour scheme. There is a total of twelve possible analogous schemes, each centred on one of the twelve basic hues.

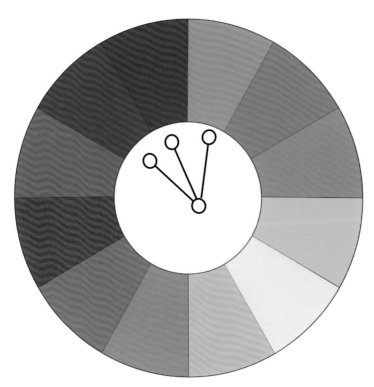

The colour
schemes
work by
going from
left to
right in a
line.

615C	127C	141C
127C	141C	7410C
141C	7410C	486C
615	486C	710C
486C	710C	695C
710C	695C	7662C
695C	7662C	272C
7662C	272C	7689C
272C	7689C	7549C
7689C	7549C	346C
7549C	346C	615C
346C	615C	127C

Complimentary colour schemes

Alternatively, you may want a contrast to your colours. To obtain maximum hue contrast between two colours, you would choose colours directly opposite each another on the circle. This is called a complementary colour scheme because the two colours compliment each other. Again it is essential to use the colour wheel for reference, as this only works by selecting the colours that are directly opposite each other in the colour wheel. There are six possible complementary pairs.

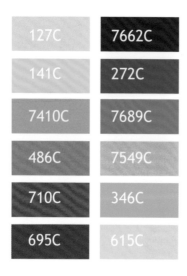

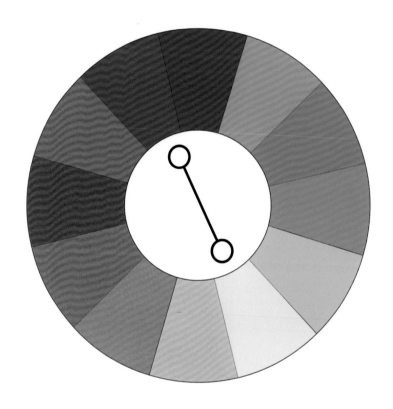

Triadic colour scheme

If you wanted the maximum contrast in your colour scheme you would choose three contrasting colours that are equidistant on the circle. (Four colour spaces apart). This is called a triadic colour scheme. There are four possible triadic colour combinations.

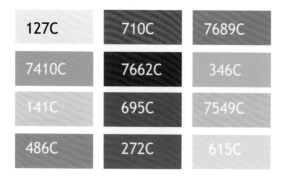

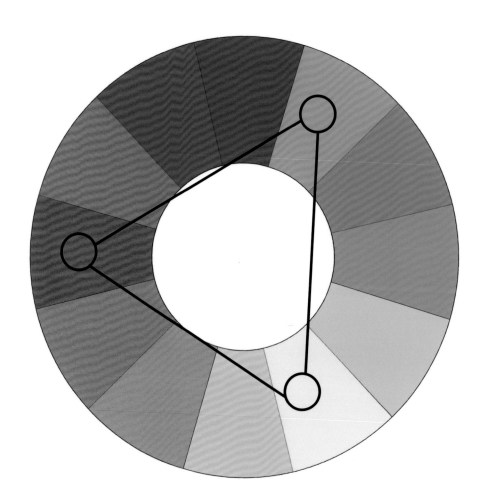

Spilt complimentary colour schemes

Like the complimentary colour scheme from page 56, this combination allows you to choose a direct opposite of colour in contrast. But instead of selecting the direct opposite - you simply choose the neighbouring colours either side, meaning you now have three colours to your colour scheme.

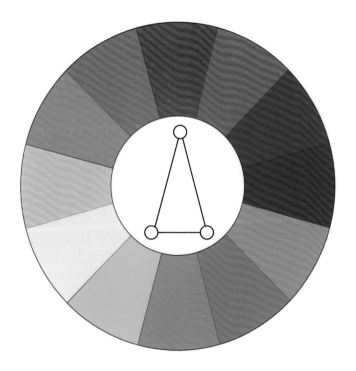

272C	127C	695C
7689C	141C	7662C
7549C	7410C	272C
346C	486C	7689C
615C	710C	7549C
127C	695C	346C
141C	7662C	615C
7410C	272C	127C
141C	7689C	486C
7410C	7549C	710C
486C	346C	695C
710C	615C	7662C

Rectangle colour scheme

The rectangle or tetradic colour scheme uses four colours. It looks more complicated than it is - if I break the different elements of the rectangle down you will see how the four colours are selected. It is simply, 2 sets of complimentary pairs. (With one colour space in between them). There are 11 combinations of rectangle colour schemes.

615 C	141 C	695C	272 C
127 C	7410 C	7662 C	7689 C
141 C	686 C	272 C	7549 C
7410 C	710 C	7689 C	346 C
486 C	695 C	7549 C	615 C
710 C	7662 C	346 C	127 C
695 C	272 C	615 C	141 C
7662 C	7689 C	127C	7410 C
272 C	7549 C	141 C	486 C
7689 C	346 C	7410 C	710 C
7549 C	615 C	486 C	695 C

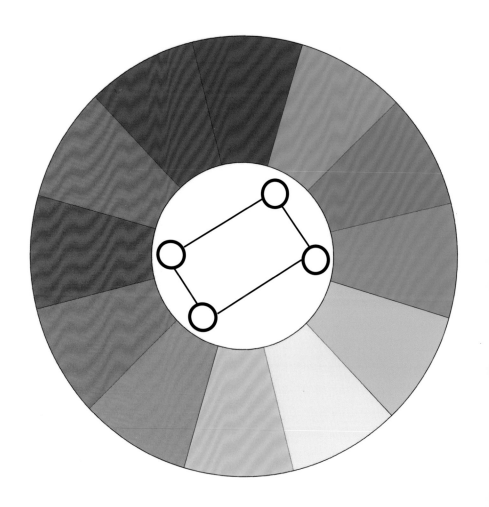

Square colour scheme

This is obviously similar to the rectangle, it contains four colours but this time they are evenly spaced around the colour wheel. (So two colour spaces between each selection). There are 12 square colour scheme combinations.

615 C	141 C	710 C	7689 C
127 C	7410 C	695 C	7549 C
141 C	486 C	7662 C	346 C
7410 C	710 C	272 C	615 C
486 C	695 C	7689 C	127 C
710 C	7662 C	7549 C	141 C
695 C	272 C	346 C	7410 C
7662 C	7689 C	615 C	486 C
272 C	7549 C	127 C	710 C
7689 C	346 C	141 C	695 C
7549 C	615 C	7410 C	7662 C
346 C	127 C	486 C	272 C

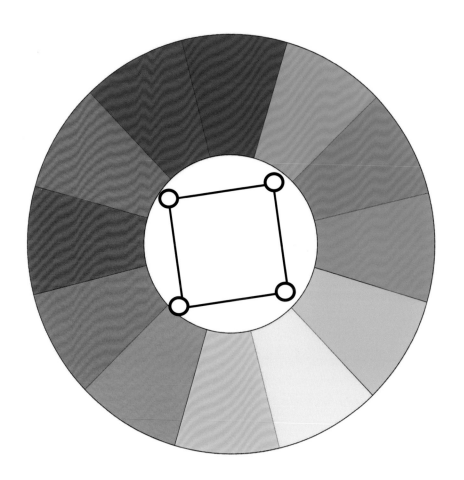

Using them to best effect:

It's all very well knowing how to select a colour scheme, (and trust me so many people don't) but using them correctly is the next battle in creating that perfect cake. Whilst I have helped you on your way to creating a visually stunning cake, it's up to you now to look at HOW you use them and still retain a good balance of the colours you have selected. For most colour scheme choices it is important to let one colour dominate and to use the same hue (saturation of colour). It is also important to pay attention to the use of cold and warm colours in your chosen colour scheme, as these can completely alter the look or feel that you are going for.

Warm colours

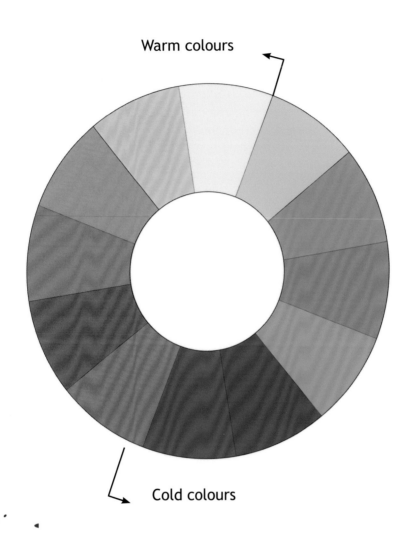

Cold colours

My colour inspiration

Inspiration for a cake can come from anywhere. I find so much of my colour inspiration comes from nature. Take a look at these images and then when you're out and about start snapping. Collect and store them in here for your future creations.

The mix of blues and greens is stunning, Mixed with the contrasting brown rock face and darker blue sky makes it appealing to the eye.

Even in nature, vibrant contrasts really work well.

Who can resist a pile of autumn leaves.... This one is vibrant with it's mix of reds and oranges.

I couldn't resist the colours of this succulent wreath, the most amazing and unusual combination of green and purples.

Over to You!

Here is some space to record your own colour recipes. At home I use the left columns of the table to record the colour name, (if I give it one) and the ratios of colours, and the final column to spray the actual colour mixed as a visual reference. I mask off the other lines in the table with paper or card before spraying so as to not affect any other colours I have recorded.

Useful tips!

When recording your colours, Don't spray too much, too close you run the risk of saturating the paper and ruining your book!

Once the page is full, why not cover it with sticky-back plastic sheets to protect it!

Make yourself a stencil! Cover the table with acetate then trace one of the right hand column boxes.Carefully cut out with a craft knife and use it when recording your colour creations!

Colour Name	Colour Ratio Mix	Colour Outcome

Colour Name	Colour Ratio Mix	Colour Outcome

Colour Name	Colour Ratio Mix	Colour Outcome

Colour Name	Colour Ratio Mix	Colour Outcome

Dinkydoodle Ready-made Colour Range

Whilst I may add to the range of colours and finishes available to buy in the future there will always be a selection of colours that form my "essential" range. These are the colours that ALL of the colours in this book were derived from, so when I refer to a Dinkydoodle yellow, red or pink for example, I am referring to these ready-made colours that are available to buy.

Don't forget some of these are also available in a pearl or iridescent finish, and there is also my gold, pearl, copper and bronze!

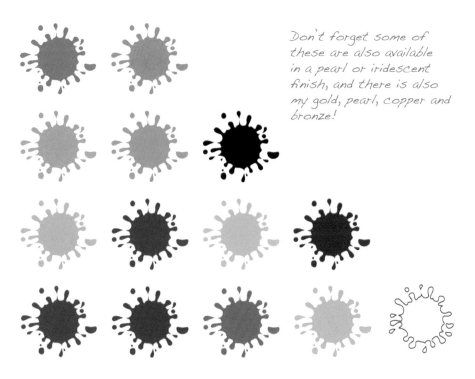

Notes

Notes

Notes